GUIDELINES

Guidelines for

MW01114314

GUIDELINES

Women's
Ministries

*Turning Faith, Hope,
and Love into Action*

United Methodist Women

WOMEN'S MINISTRIES

Some paragraph numbers for and language in the Book of Discipline *and the* Book of Resolutions *may have changed in the 2012 revision, which was published after these Guidelines were printed. We regret any inconvenience.*

Contents

Called to a Ministry of Faithfulness and Vitality

Y ou are so important to the life of the Christian church! You have consented to join with other people of faith who, through the millennia, have sustained the church by extending God's love to others. You have been called and have committed your unique passions, gifts, and abilities to a position of leadership. This Guideline will help you understand the basic elements of that ministry within your own church and within The United Methodist Church.

Leadership in Vital Ministry

Each person is called to ministry by virtue of his or her baptism, and that ministry takes place in all aspects of daily life, both in and outside of the church. Your leadership role requires that you will be a faithful participant in the **mission of the church**, which is to partner with God to **make disciples of Jesus Christ for the transformation of the world**. You will not only engage in your area of ministry, but will also work to empower others to be in ministry as well. The vitality of your church, and the Church as a whole, depends upon the faith, abilities, and actions of all who work together for the glory of God.

Clearly then, as a pastoral leader or leader among the laity, your ministry is not just a "job," but a spiritual endeavor. You are a spiritual leader now, and others will look to you for spiritual leadership. What does this mean?

All persons who follow Jesus are called to grow spiritually through the practice of various Christian habits (or "means of grace") such as prayer, Bible study, private and corporate worship, acts of service, Christian conferencing, and so on. Jesus taught his disciples practices of spiritual growth and leadership that you will model as you guide others. As members of the congregation grow through the means of grace, they will assume their own role in ministry and help others in the same way. This is the cycle of disciple making.

The Church's Vision

While there is one mission—to make disciples of Jesus Christ—the portrait of a successful mission will differ from one congregation to the next. One of your roles is to listen deeply for the guidance and call of God in your own context. In your church, neighborhood, or greater community, what are the greatest needs? How is God calling your congregation to be in a ministry of service and witness where they are? What does vital ministry look like in the life of your congregation and its neighbors? What are the characteristics, traits, and actions that identify a person as a faithful disciple in your context?

This portrait, or vision, is formed when you and the other leaders discern together how your gifts from God come together to fulfill the will of God.

Assessing Your Efforts

We are generally good at deciding what to do, but we sometimes skip the more important first question of what we want to accomplish. Knowing your task (the mission of disciple making) and knowing what results you want (the vision of your church) are the first two steps in a vital ministry. The third step is in knowing how you will assess or measure the results of what you do and who you are (and become) because of what you do. Those measures relate directly to mission and vision, and they are more than just numbers.

One of your leadership tasks will be to take a hard look, with your team, at all the things your ministry area does or plans to do. No doubt they are good and worthy activities; the question is, *"Do these activities and experiences lead people into a mature relationship with God and a life of deeper discipleship?"* That is the business of the church, and the church needs to do what only the church can do. You may need to eliminate or alter some of what you do if it does not measure up to the standard of faithful disciple making. It will be up to your ministry team to establish the specific standards against which you compare all that you do and hope to do. (This Guideline includes further help in establishing goals, strategies, and measures for this area of ministry.)

The Mission of The United Methodist Church

Each local church is unique, yet it is a part of a *connection,* a living organism of the body of Christ. Being a connectional Church means in part that all United Methodist churches are interrelated through the structure and organization of districts, conferences, and jurisdictions in the larger "family" of the denomination. *The Book of Discipline of The United Methodist Church* describes, among other things, the ministry of all United Methodist Christians, the essence of servant ministry and leadership, how to organize and accomplish that ministry, and how our connectional structure works (see especially ¶¶126–138).

Our Church extends way beyond your doorstep; it is a global Church with both local and international presence. You are not alone. The resources of the entire denomination are intended to assist you in ministry. With this help and the partnership of God and one another, the mission continues. You are an integral part of God's church and God's plan!

(For help in addition to this Guideline and the *Book of Discipline*, see "Resources" at the end of your Guideline, www.umc.org, and the other websites listed on the inside back cover.)

Introduction: United Methodist Women in Mission

United Methodist Women is a faith-based membership organization of laywomen within The United Methodist Church. Members are committed to growing as disciples of Jesus Christ in community with other women and building the lives of people forced into the margins of society. United Methodist Women has been in mission with women, children, and youth for more than 140 years.

United Methodist Women and its predecessor mission organizations have advocated for justice consistently, giving support to full clergy rights for women, establishment of the United Nations (U.N.), Universal Declaration of Human Rights and founding of the World Council of Churches.

In recent years, United Methodist Women members have been working for racial and economic justice, fair labor practices, immigrant and refugee rights, stewardship of the environment, rights for victims of domestic violence and human trafficking, and for peace.

Currently, the organization has approximately 800,000 members who raised more than $17 million for the entire program of United Methodist Women in 2010. United Methodist Women extends advocacy, service and leadership training to women, children and youth in partnership with 97 national mission institutions, about 300 international projects in 80 countries, seven regional missionaries, 18 Persons in Mission, 159 deaconesses and 10 home missioners. Members equip themselves for mission through spiritual growth, mission education, and training.

You too can become a part of this growing and evolving sisterhood of grace and actively participate in God's mission in the world with thousands of United Methodist Women sisters!

What Is the PURPOSE?

United Methodist Women is a community of women whose PURPOSE is to know God and to experience freedom as whole persons through Jesus Christ; to develop a creative supportive fellowship; and to expand concepts of mission through participation in the global ministries of the church.

What Does It Mean to Be a Member of United Methodist Women?

When you join a local organization of United Methodist Women you experience many joys of membership in your personal and corporate life. United Methodist Women brings women together to grow in faith, hope, and love in action.

- **Spiritual growth**: Experience personal transformation as you deepen your relationship with Christ through prayer and study and participate in spiritual retreats.
- **Hands-on mission:** Engage in local missions through time, talent, and gifts.
- **Education for mission:** Learn and grow in understanding of mission including mission as advocacy for justice.
- **Leadership opportunities and training:** Lead and serve at local, district, conference, and jurisdiction levels. Receive face-to-face and online training. Draw on your training to serve the needs of your church and community.
- **Fellowship in small groups and programs:** Enjoy friendship and support of other sisters in Christ through participation in meetings, Bible studies, events, and projects.
- **Mission Giving:** Pledge support to work with women, children, and youth and discover how your dollars make a difference in your neighborhood and around the world.
- **Partnership:** Become a part of a community of women in mission in the country and globally.
- **Social Action network:** Get involved in social justice issues, the environment, domestic violence, immigration, and the many other concerns that impact the lives of women, children, and youth.
- **Mission resources:** Start using mission studies, **response** magazine, Program Book and Prayer Calendar to engage you in mission.
- **Reading Program:** Participate in the Reading Program and read member-reviewed books to challenge your thinking on cutting-edge issues and deepen your understanding of mission.
- **Outreach:** Use printed and Web tools for outreach to new and nonmembers.
- **Mission connections:** Remain connected in mission with the General Board of Global Ministries through our work at the U.N., Mission u, and

initiatives for mission. Partner with Church Women United and
Ecumenical Women.
- **Membership:** Become a member of the official national mission organ-
ization of women of The United Methodist Church.
- **Online community:** Enjoy friendships, discussions and ideas on
UMWOnline, United Methodist Women's social network for members,
Facebook, and Twitter.
- **Make a difference:** Engage in racial justice and transform the places
we live into antiracist, multicultural communities.

Organizing for Mission

Like The United Methodist Church, United Methodist Women has local,
district, conference, and jurisdiction structures. These organized bodies are
determined by the boundaries set by the church.

Mission is the focus at each step of the way. Leadership teams determine
the work of mission for their organization and structure accordingly.

There is no one-size-fits-all when it comes to local unit, circle, or group of
United Methodist Women. The new streamlined structures are designed to
free up members of United Methodist Women to form themselves as they
see fit in order to do the work of mission by role or responsibilities or how-
ever best serves their ability to work toward the PURPOSE.

The only titles that need to be used in all levels of the organization are president, treasurer, secretary, and committee on nominations. The rest of the
work of the team—including spiritual growth, advocacy, service, education,
leadership development, fundraising, supplying needed program materials,
informing members and nonmembers about the work of mission, inviting
new members, and establishing new units and circles—can be shared
among as many people as the unit decides, and can be organized in many
ways.

As you begin planning at the local level, your district president can be of
help to you, so feel free to call on her or another member of the district mission team. Check your conference website for contact information. The
New Unit Starter Kit listed in the Resources section is also a useful tool for
you.

Join a local organization today or start one in your church and be a part of
the ever-widening circle of United Methodist Women.

What Is the Foundation of United Methodist Women?

U nited Methodist Women members are in mission in response to God's grace. Their foundational goals to know and worship God, grow as disciples in community with other sisters and engage in and equip for mission to extend wholeness to all are key to United Methodist Women's PURPOSE and are also emphasized in the 2011 Call to Action report. The United Methodist Church's Call to Action report provides guidelines for the revitalization of the church.

The United Methodist Women Living the Vision for 2010–2020 sharpens the PURPOSE of United Methodist Women and energizes its vision in order to remain vital in the years to come:

The Vision
Turning faith, hope, and love into action on behalf of women, children, and youth around the world.

Living the Vision
We provide opportunities and resources to grow spiritually, become more deeply rooted in Christ, and put faith into action.

We are organized for growth, with flexible structures leading to effective witness and action.

We equip women and girls around the world to be leaders in communities, agencies, workplaces. governments, and churches.

We work for justice through compassionate service and advocacy to change unfair policies and systems.

We provide educational experiences that lead to personal change in order to transform the world.

What Is the Emblem?

t he emblem of United Methodist Women is symbolic of our organization. The cross and flame are ancient symbols of the church and also appear on The United Methodist Church emblem. Both symbols remind us of the opportunities and obligation of discipleship.

Paul's words to Timothy have fresh and new meanings: "I remind you to stir into flame the gift of God which is within you" (2 Timothy 1:6 NEB). As United Methodist Women we share our gift of God with others through mission.

United
Methodist
Women
FAITH · HOPE · LOVE IN ACTION

As parts of our emblem, the cross and flame remind us of our PURPOSE of growing in our understanding of and willingness to participate in the global ministries of the church. They remind us of our heritage of women who pioneer in service for the church at home and in other countries.

The overall shape of the emblem is also symbolic. Fluid and free flowing, the shape suggests change and mobility. The women who came before us were at the forefront of movements for change. Always aware of the times, we move with ever changing circumstances rather than feeling overwhelmed by them. We are a group of Christian women with many gifts who are unified by one Spirit. We participate in God's mission in all areas of life.

In 2010, the board of directors added a summary of the vision to the emblem. Together, they remind us of how and why we organize for mission.

What Is the Identity of United Methodist Women?

History

From the beginning women's mission work has been visionary and dedicated.

BEGINNINGS

In the late 1800s, the women of the Methodist and Evangelical Brethren traditions each came to realize that they needed to organize themselves for service to others during this period when women and children were considered nonpersons in society.

In 1869, a small group of women in the Methodist Episcopal Church decided to organize themselves into what became the Woman's Foreign Missionary Society. This was the beginning of service and mission work in all the predecessor organizations that has expanded from:

The Boston Six

- Two missionaries in India to work in more than 80 countries.
- Three hundred dollars to millions of dollars for the program of United Methodist Women.
- Six women gathering in Boston, Mass., in 1869 to more than 7,000 gathering in St. Louis, Mo., in 2010 to celebrate and affirm the work of United Methodist Women at Assembly.

MERGERS

The organization of United Methodist Women has evolved from 11 women's mission groups of predecessor churches. Each of these groups was formed to serve women and children. Through reorganization and denominational mergers these groups were brought together. In 1973, United Methodist Women became the name of the women's mission organization of The United Methodist Church.

LEADERS

The organization of United Methodist Women has been influenced by the strength and spirituality of courageous women in what has become The United Methodist Church.

Clementina Butler and Lois Parker
The Woman's Foreign Missionary Society of the Methodist Episcopal Church was formed in Boston, Mass., in 1869 at the motivation of Clementina Butler and Lois Parker, wives of two missionaries serving in India.

Clementina Butler

Lois Parker

Lizzie Hoffman
Lizzie Hoffman was instrumental in helping organize the Woman's Missionary Association of the United Brethren Church. In 1875, Ms. Hoffman and a group of concerned women got together in Dayton, Ohio, and issued a call for a Woman's Missionary Convention. Out of that meeting the Woman's Missionary Association was formed.

Virginia Laskey
Virginia Laskey served as the fourth national president of the Woman's Division of Christian Service from 1964 to 1968. At the end of her presidency, the Woman's Division established a $50,000 scholarship fund for theological education for women in her honor. Scarritt College in Nashville, Tenn., now Scarritt-Bennett Center, also honored her by

naming its library the Laskey Library. She was an outspoken advocate of a just society and a racially inclusive church.

Mai H. Gray

Mai H. Gray grew up in Jackson, Tenn. She was a member of the "Committee of 24" that proposed the organizational structure for United Methodist Women in 1972. Also in 1972, Ms. Gray was elected a member of the Women's Division board of directors. From 1976 to 1980, she served as the division's first black president. The division honored her presidency by establishing the Mai H. Gray Education Grant to Women and Children in Zimbabwe, Namibia, and South Africa.

Thelma Stevens

A native of Mississippi, Thelma Stevens graduated from State Teachers' College at Hattiesburg, Miss., now the University of Southern Mississippi. In 1926, Ms. Stevens entered Scarritt College for Christian Workers in Nashville, Tenn., completing a master's degree in 1928. From 1928 to 1940, Ms. Stevens served as director of the Bethlehem Center in Augusta, Ga. Ms. Stevens held the position of executive secretary for the Department of Christian Social Relations and Local Church Activities with the Woman's Division and then the Women's Division from 1940 until her retirement in 1968. Ms. Stevens is best remembered for her untiring efforts toward the elimination of racism in the church and society.

Theressa Hoover

A native of Fayetteville, Ark., Theressa Hoover attended Philander Smith College in Little Rock, Ark. Upon graduation, Ms. Hoover accepted the position of associate director with the Little Rock Methodist Council. In 1948 she went to work for the Woman's Division as a fieldworker. For 10 years Ms. Hoover traveled among the woman's societies attending and resourcing districts, conferences and jurisdiction meetings and maintaining contact with leaders across the connection. Ms. Hoover moved to New York City in 1958 when she became staff member of the Woman's Division's Department of Christian Social Relations. In 1965 she became assistant general secretary, Section of Program and Education for Christian Mission, Woman's Division. In 1968 she was chosen to head the Women's Division as its deputy general secretary, a position she held until her retirement in December 1990.

Today, the United Methodist Women continues to be led by dedicated and capable lay women leaders. Inelda González, president, led the United Methodist Women during the last quadrennium. Harriett Jane Olson serves as general secretary/chief executive officer.

*Harriett Jane Olson
(Photo: Kristina Krug)*

*Inelda González
(Photo: Kristina Krug)*

United Methodist Women's Assembly, St. Louis, Mo., 2010 (Photo: Cassandra Zampini)

United Methodist Women Language Ministries Voices Event, Nashville, Tenn., 2010 (Photo: Kristina Krug)

HISTORICAL CHART OF UNITED METHODIST WOMEN

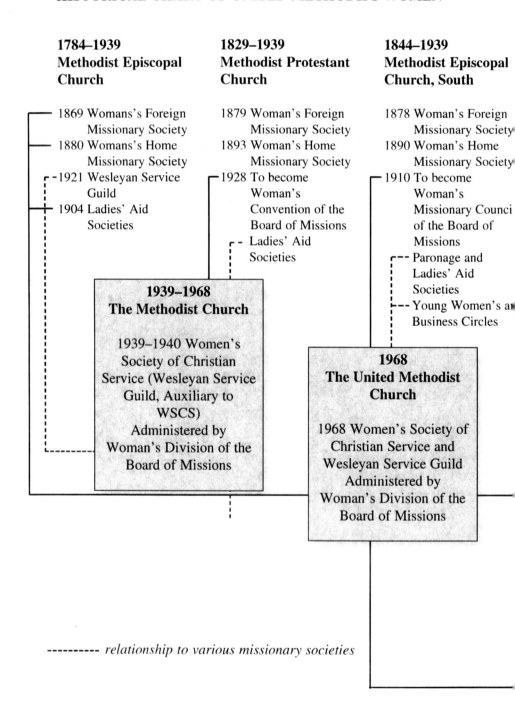

1784–1939
Methodist Episcopal
Church

1869 Womans's Foreign
Missionary Society
1880 Womans's Home
Missionary Society
1921 Wesleyan Service
Guild
1904 Ladies' Aid
Societies

1829–1939
Methodist Protestant
Church

1879 Woman's Foreign
Missionary Society
1893 Woman's Home
Missionary Society
1928 To become
Woman's
Convention of the
Board of Missions
Ladies' Aid
Societies

1844–1939
Methodist Episcopal
Church, South

1878 Woman's Foreign
Missionary Society
1890 Woman's Home
Missionary Society
1910 To become
Woman's
Missionary Council
of the Board of
Missions
Paronage and
Ladies' Aid
Societies
Young Women's a
Business Circles

1939–1968
The Methodist Church

1939–1940 Women's
Society of Christian
Service (Wesleyan Service
Guild, Auxiliary to
WSCS)
Administered by
Woman's Division of the
Board of Missions

1968
The United Methodist
Church

1968 Women's Society of
Christian Service and
Wesleyan Service Guild
Administered by
Woman's Division of the
Board of Missions

---------- *relationship to various missionary societies*

HISTORICAL CHART OF UNITED METHODIST WOMEN

1800–1946
United Brethren in Christ

1875 Womans's Missionary Association
1909 Administrative responsibilities
merged with General Home and
Foreign Service Missionary
Societies
--- Harford Circle (for Business
Women)
--- Otterbien Circle (for Young Women)

1803–1922
Evangelical Association
United Evangelical Church

1922–1946
Evangelical Church

1884 Womans's Missionary Society
--- Christian Service Guild
(for Business Women)
--- Young People's Missionary Circle
(prior to formation of EYF in 1942)

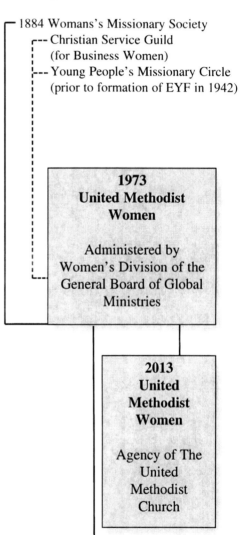

1946–1968
Evangelical United
Brethren Church

1946 Women's Society of
World Service Christian
Service Guild combined to
become in 1958 Women's
Society of World Service
Administered by
Women's Division of the
Board of Missions

1973
United Methodist
Women

Administered by
Women's Division of the
General Board of Global
Ministries

2013
United
Methodist
Women

Agency of The
United
Methodist
Church

Structure

United Methodist Women is organized and structured for mission.

The United Methodist Church through its General Conference provides for an organization of United Methodist Women from the local to the national level. *The Book of Discipline of The United Methodist Church,* ¶ 256 states: "In every local church there shall be an organized unit of United Methodist Women. The name of this organization shall be United Methodist Women. The unit of United Methodist Women in the local church is directly related to the district, conference and national organizations of United Methodist Women." If your local church does not currently have a United Methodist Women's group you can organize one, become a member at a near-by church, or join or organize a group at the district level.

United Methodist Women elects its own leaders to a board of directors and the national organization is incorporated as a nonprofit organization. United Methodist Women raises funds every year for mission including mission education. This is also authorized in *The Book of Discipline.*

From 1964–2012 the national policymaking body of the United Methodist Women has been called Women's Division, a division of the General Board of Global Ministries of The United Methodist Church. In 2012, United Methodist Women became an agency of The United Methodist Church fulfilling its PURPOSE in the world guided by its vision and outcomes; and reporting directly to the General Conference while working alongside the General Board of Global Ministries.

Work

The entire program of United Methodist Women is mission. United Methodist Women members join in God's mission as they are transformed by their relationship with God through prayer, study, and the empowering of the Holy Spirit. They equip themselves for mission through education and leadership training, learn about and raise awareness of justice issues, and engage in service and advocacy on behalf of women, children, and youth in the United States and around the world. Mission Giving undergirds the mission program.

ADVOCACY AND SERVICE

The national body of the United Methodist Women is specifically charged with being "an advocate for the oppressed and dispossessed with special attention to the needs of women and children" (*The Book of Discipline,* 2008, ¶ 1319). The organization provides resources and opportunities for members to help improve the lives of women, children, and youth nationally and internationally through both advocacy and direct service. Women, children, and youth are considered not only as objects of our concern but also subjects of their own lives and futures.

The work of pursuing racial and economic justice and peace is an ongoing task of the prophetic ministry of United Methodist Women to transform the world for women and children. Just as women in the most vulnerable communities in the global village continue to struggle for equity in the work place, rights to adequate health care, access to needed services, and elimination of all forms of gender-based discrimination and safety from all forms of violence, women in the so-called "developed" countries also face barriers in some of the same areas. Our advocacy work continues its course building on 140 years of service.

Over the years, United Methodist Women has identified various emphases to focus on. Our current priority areas emphasize issues emerging from immigration, climate change, domestic violence and human trafficking, especially where these issues have a disparate impact on women and children.

Christian Social Action
Advocacy allows us to be transformers by calling us to change the systems that exclude women, eliminate barriers to women's progress and to be proactive in our efforts. Compassionate service takes us to where the hurt and pain is and gives us a glimpse of God's image in all God's people.

United Methodist Women's offices in Washington, D.C. and New York engage in advocacy on issues that most affect women, children, and youth. Programming by the following ministries focuses on advocacy and service on a daily basis:

Church Center for United Nations
United Methodist Women, the General Board of Global Ministries and the General Board of Church and Society carry together a long legacy of support for the development of instruments of international peace and cooperation, education and advocacy through the work at the Church Center for the United Nations (CCUN).

Established in the 1960s, CCUN continues to serve as a door of access for the nongovernmental ecumenical and interfaith community to the U.N. Many churches and religious organizations have their office to the U.N. in this building.

Nongovernmental organization (NGO) working groups, including the Ecumenical Working Group, Ecumenical Women, Office of the Chaplain of this Church Center, and the World Council of Churches, gather prior to and during U.N. conferences to critique and offer input in the drafting process of U.N. resolutions and conventions, monitor the work of the U.N. agencies and member states, and lift up voices of those on the margins of society.

United Methodist Women works closely with Ecumenical Women to organize parallel events and host delegations particularly for events like the annual Commission on the Status of Women meetings. We continue to support and participate in the work of the indigenous peoples' rights movement at the U.N.

Another important ministry of CCUN is that of hospitality. The center offers desk space and office facilities to groups and individuals advocating for human rights. Tillman Chapel offers space for prayer and meditation.

The United Methodist Office for the United Nations (UMOUN) comprised of United Methodist Women and General Board of Church and Society provides educational opportunities through its Seminar Program bringing church members from across the globe to experience conflict resolution and advocacy toward reconciliation. This program engages more than a thousand youth and adults every year on key issues such as the Middle East, peacemaking, immigration, globalization and poverty, and more.

Likewise, United Methodist Women's national and international ministries offer services, counseling, and advocacy for social justice seeking to empower those served.

National Ministries
National Mission Institutions
United Methodist Women through their Mission Giving support National Mission Institutions. These 97 institutions are located across the United States—schools, colleges, community centers, women's residences, and treatment centers. They offer a variety of services and work with communities to meet emerging needs.

Deaconess and Home Missioner Program
Deaconesses have been a part of our tradition as a church since 1888, and at the 2004 General Conference the Home Missioner program was established to provide laymen with an opportunity to serve in a lifetime relationship in The United Methodist Church. For much of its history the office of deaconess was associated with the women's organizations. In 1964, the Board of Mission (later General Board of Global Ministries) began their responsibility for this office, and in 2010 it was assigned to the national organization

of United Methodist Women. In some ways of thinking, the deaconesses have "come home" and United Methodist Women are very happy to be more closely connected.

As servants of the church in the world, deaconesses and home missioners commit to a lifetime professional vocation led by the Spirit of God in ministries of love, justice, and service. Deaconesses and home missioners of The United Methodist Church earnestly seek to carry forward their ministry in sincerity and in love under the direction of the church. Their ministry is often with those who are most marginalized, representing the love and concern of the believing community for the needs of the world. The motto of deaconesses and home missioners is "I serve neither for gratitude nor reward but from gratitude and love; my reward is that I may serve." Together as a mutually supportive covenant community, they are one expression of the ecumenical world diaconate that reaches out in service to all parts of the earth.

International Ministries
Global Justice Volunteers Program
The Global Justice Volunteers Program arose from a recognized need to develop opportunities for young adults as part of an overall effort to broaden volunteer mission opportunities.

This program enables young adults who are 18–30 years old to have short-term mission experiences, living and learning alongside people whose lives are shaped by justice work. The program provides opportunities for service, learning, and cross-cultural exposure. Through this program, individuals explore the links between faith and justice through mission work.

Bible Women Program
The Bible Women Program is based on an historical program of the same name that was initiated in 1869 by the Woman's Foreign Missionary Society. Today, the Bible Women Program draws on the original design of bringing leadership training and development to the marginalized in both remote rural and urban areas. Through a participatory method, women work with trainers to set a course of study in areas that focus on Bible study, literacy, health/nutrition, economic development, and an understanding of human/women's rights.

Regional Missionary Initiative
The Regional Missionary Initiative was developed in response to requests for leadership and organizational development from Methodist and United Methodist women around the world.

Regional missionaries work in their assigned areas to assist women, children, and youth to work in solidarity with one another on specific issues. Regional missionaries build relationships with Methodist, United Methodist, ecumenical, and grassroots programs that focus on issues of health, gender equality and elimination of violence among women and support for the uprooted and marginalized.

Ubuntu Journeys

Ubuntu Journeys are unique, short-term mission service opportunities for United Methodist Women to interact with the world through mission partners. These journeys are about women of faith coming together through shared mission to address social issues and discover new ways of working together, supporting one another and growing spiritually. Together with global sisters, United Methodist Women share the experience of worship, prayer, and spiritual reflection and engage in mission that will cultivate faith, hope, and love into action.

EDUCATING FOR MISSION AND EQUIPPING FOR LEADERSHIP

Mission education fuels not only spiritual growth of United Methodist Women members but also spurs their involvement with advocacy and service. As an organization in the Wesleyan tradition, United Methodist Women believes that these are inseparable. Women are also equipped for leadership through several training opportunities during the year.

Schools of Christian Mission (now Mission u: Learning Together for the Transformation of the World)

Schools of Christian Mission were started in the mid-1930s by the Woman's Home Missionary Society. The schools are organized by United Methodist Women leaders in each conference of The United Methodist Church. In some conferences, United Methodist Women partners with the conference agency responsible for mission to implement the schools, which in turn relates with the General Board of Global Ministries. Every year more than 20,000 people participate in these schools.

Mission u are opportunities to study mission topics based on current issues impacting society. Each year selected themes related to a spiritual growth topic, a geographic area, and a current issue are developed into mission studies. These are the focus of study at each school. Check your conference website for information.

Seminar Program on National and International Affairs

As part of the call to mission, United Methodist Women engages in justice education, learning about peace, the environment, family advocacy, public education, domestic violence, human trafficking, racial justice, global policy, and U.S. public policy. Special work on topics of their choice is made available to participants through the Seminar Program on National and International Affairs at the Church Center for United Nations in New York City.

Leadership Development Opportunities
Leadership training is central to our mission. Every year United Methodist Women members participate in training with the unique focus of expanding their skills, knowledge, and abilities for a deeper understanding of mission and service.

Training for the members of United Methodist Women is available in a variety of contexts. Training is developed specifically for officers and persons in leadership positions in the organization. Check with conference president or mission team for information on training events.

Scholarships
International and national scholarships are offered each year to equip women to become leaders.

MEMBERSHIP OUTREACH
United Methodist Women is the official women's organization of The United Methodist Church. Its membership is voluntary and open to all women committed and engaged in mission.

"Membership shall be open to any woman who indicates her desire to belong and to participate in the global mission of the church through United Methodist Women. The pastor(s) shall be an ex-officio member of the local unit and of its executive committee" (*The Book of Discipline of The United Methodist Church*, 2008, ¶ 256).

By building a community of women committed to mission—with members in every local United Methodist Church—United Methodist Women is expanding programs and concepts of mission.

Organizing women's groups in new church starts, equipping and collaborating with language coordinators, and hosting and mentoring young women's events and groups are some ways women are participating in God's mission.

We invite you to join this creative, supportive fellowship of women of all ages, ethnicities, social, and educational backgrounds with the common goal of participating in God's mission through witness and work.

MISSION GIVING

"As an organization, United Methodist Women has not merely sent money from a distance...they have always understood giving as an expression of God's grace. Their faith has led them to follow the gospel and to support the mission and ministry of Jesus" (A Policy Statement on Giving, p. 1). Not all members of the United Methodist Women can travel the world, but their mission dollars can and do through the five channels of Mission Giving locally, nationally, and internationally.

Women prayerfully make pledges to their local organization or district. Their Mission Giving goes toward local mission, spiritual formation, programs for membership development, and outreach in the community. Each local organization of United Methodist Women also assigns a pledge to mission to be sent to their district. The process is repeated at district and conference levels. The pledged amount designated for mission is sent to the national body. Your pledge underwrites our entire network of training and national and international mission. Women are involved in mission each step of the way.

Five Channels of Giving
Pledge to Mission
This is the largest channel of Mission Giving. Local women pledge and raise funds through various methods, and their local treasurer sends on funds to support the foundational work of United Methodist Women.

Special Mission Recognition
An individual, circle, or any group of United Methodist Women may recognize a faithful worker in mission by giving her or him a Special Mission Recognition pin. There are several categories of pins to choose from—each one represents a different level of mission giving. Contact your conference treasurer for information.

Gift to Mission
A wide variety of mission cards are available for purchase singly or in prepackaged sets for different occasions to honor someone: Peace, Thank-You, Congratulations, Thinking of You, A Special Day, A New Baby, In the Service of Christ, Happy Birthday, and Christmas.

Gift in Memory
A Gift in Memory card represents a gift to mission through the United Methodist Women and makes additional mission work possible in the United States and around the world.

World Thank Offering
Offerings of gratitude are taken during the annual World Thank Offering service.

Grants
United Methodist Women members also give special offerings that are designated toward grants.

Brighter Future for Children and Youth
United Methodist Women offers grants of up to $4,000 for projects and programs addressing the needs of children and young people between the ages of 5 and 18 in the areas of violence prevention, anti-abuse, and relationship abuse.

Brighter Future grants are those that
- Cultivate spiritual life and values.
- Provide direct and comprehensive services to young people.
- Demonstrate the ability to raise additional funds from other sources.
- Include significant involvement of women and youth at grass-roots level.
- Promote respect for and appreciation of racial and ethnic diversity.

Call to Prayer and Self-Denial
This annual observance gives local and district organizations an opportunity to study and reflect on a particular theme each year and to designate funds for ministries related to the theme for the year. Offerings from the Call to Prayer and Self-Denial, totaling nearly one million, provide support for mission through grants and dedicated gifts to programs with women, children and youth.

Major and Planned Giving
Through major and planned giving United Methodist Women extends faith, hope and love into the future. A member of United Methodist Women can ensure that the mission work she cares passionately about continues into the future by considering naming United Methodist Women in her Will or using another approach to major or planned gift.

Major gifts are significant donations made on an occasional or one-time basis to support an organization, often for a capital campaign or special fund-raising drive. Major gifts may be paid out over a period of years. Major gifts are often restricted by the donor. A planned gift is often deferred, meaning that the gift (such as a bequest, life insurance policy, or pooled-income fund) is not available for use until a future time, usually on the death of the donor and the disposition of the donor's estate.

Over more than 140 years of women organized for mission, our generous predecessors have left planned gifts both small and large so that mission work would continue long after their deaths. There are some 650 endowments in the care of our national organization for work ranging from "foreign missions" to "Bible women, India" to "specialized training, deaconesses and other workers" to "the educational and medical work of the United Methodist Women or wherever most needed."

Who We Are Within The United Methodist Church

United Methodist Women is an integral part of The United Methodist Church not only providing advocacy and service on behalf of women, children, and youth but also taking a lead role in expanding concepts of mission for the whole church. A United Methodist Women conference president is a member of her annual conference and often serves on a variety of committees. The local organization president is a member of the church administrative council.

The local United Methodist Women member usually serves in a variety of ministries, such as Sunday school, choir, prayer services, Bible studies, church lunches, homeless shelters or soup kitchens and many other activities. Being a part of United Methodist Women provides her with training to equip her as leader in her church and in her community.

Women have always banded together for the work of mission, and while the core of our work remains the same, the way we organize to best accomplish the tasks of mission has evolved. Our current organization was described in proposals presented at the General Conference of 2012, which were approved and will be included in *The Book of Discipline*, 2012.

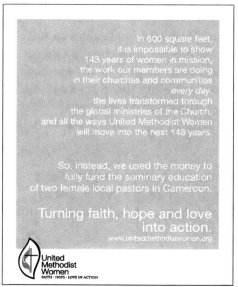

United Methodist Women poster displayed at General Conference, 2012

What's Next for United Methodist Women?

moving forward, United Methodist Women will be structurally separate from the General Board of Global Ministries (GBGM) for the first time in more than 70 years. At the same time, the two entities are affirming new and existing areas of mission connection. Organized for effective witness and action, United Methodist Women has put into place the following strategies to enable more missions possible with women, children, and youth in the years to come:

PROGRAM RESPONSIBILITIES

United Methodist Women will continue to provide opportunities and resources for spiritual growth; engage in service and advocacy; equip women and girls to be leaders; expand concepts of mission through education; reach out to members; and raise and allocate funds for accomplishing the work. In 2010, United Methodist Women assumed responsibility for the administration and funding of the Office of Deaconess and Home Missioner committing to growing the lay ministry in the church.

United Methodist Women also took direct oversight responsibility for National Mission Institutions, international projects and regional missionaries working with women, children, and youth in 2010. Regional missionaries support organization and leadership development for women, children, and youth in Methodist, United Methodist, and ecumenical settings outside the United States. Instead of providing funding to Global Ministries to use for support of missionaries generally, United Methodist Women has taken on the full funding responsibility for its regional missionaries. General Conference 2012 confirmed United Methodist Women's direct administration of this national and international work that it has funded for so long.

United Methodist Women will also continue to fund positions for local women working in Central Conferences as Persons in Mission, and contribute to board development and financial support of its National Mission institutions in the United States.

FLEXIBILITY AND CONNECTION FOR MEMBERS

United Methodist Women will provide structural connection between United Methodist Women members, their national policymaking body, and the ministries they support. Recommendations to this effect were approved by the General Conference. United Methodist Women will also be connected to United Methodist leadership through the new structure.

UNITED METHODIST WOMEN NATIONAL OFFICE
Women's Division staff will be transferred from GBGM as the named employer to United Methodist Women National Office, effective October 1, 2012. The office locations (475 Riverside Drive, 777 UN Plaza, and the Methodist Building in Washington D.C.) will remain the same.

GOVERNANCE
United Methodist Women's national policymaking body, the Women's Division, will be called United Methodist Women National Office, and its board of directors will continue to be responsible for setting budgets, policies, and raising funds for mission. The board size will be reduced from 50 members to 25 members. The board will confer with a 70- to 80-member program advisory group comprised of United Methodist Women members and mission partners. Every conference will be connected at the national level through this advisory group.

JURISDICTION, CONFERENCE, AND DISTRICT UNITED METHODIST WOMEN
Each jurisdiction, conference, and district will continue to have a corresponding level of United Methodist Women organized in accordance with the program and policies of the national organization of United Methodist Women.

District and conference United Methodist Women will elect a leadership team, including at least, but not limited to, a president, a treasurer, a secretary, and a chair of committee on nominations.

Districts and conferences will also organize mission team members, task forces, and committees they decide will help them to fulfill the PURPOSE.

LOCAL UNITED METHODIST WOMEN
At the local level, the constitution of local organizations of United Methodist Women remains the same as that of the previous quadrennium.

The only change in *The Book of Discipline*, 2008, ¶256.5, will be to update the name of the national policymaking body of United Methodist Women.

All local groups of United Methodist Women are encouraged to organize as they see fit to fulfill the PURPOSE.

How Do We Work With Others?

United Methodist Women considers mutuality to be basic to its mission as it collaborates with worldwide organizations highlighting the concerns of women, children, and youth around the world. Oppression, discrimination, injustice, abuse and violence are not just the concerns of United Methodist Women but other faith-based groups are called to action too.

Learn how you can become a part of this vast network through your organization of United Methodist Women.

World Federation of Methodist and Uniting Church Women

United Methodist Women is a member of World Federation of Methodist and Uniting Church Women, which is a fellowship of such officially recognized groups of Methodist, United, and Uniting Church Women organized in units from many nations who affirm its purpose "To Know Christ and to Make Him Known."

In its role as the voice of women in mission with women, children, and youth, United Methodist Women embraces the purpose of this organization: To be a support group for women acting as a catalyst in their faith and actions; to promote the interests of women in all areas of life, in spiritual growth, equality, development, and peace; to work toward the recognition of the equal status of women; to facilitate, encourage and actively promote leadership training for women; and to be a voice for Methodist, United, and Uniting Church women.

United Methodist Women participated in the 12th World Federation meeting in Johannesburg, South Africa in 2011. Our regional missionaries, staff, and directors took various leadership roles, and our own Judith Siaba, former member of our board of directors was elected president of the North American region of the organization at that time.

Ecumenical Women

Ecumenical Women fulfill an extraordinary legacy as a strong voice for gender equality at the U.N. Together, denominational representatives actively pursue the creation of national and international policies, which challenge structures of inequality.

Members of Ecumenical Women, including United Methodist Women, advocate not only for a few improvements but for a fundamental system change in church and state in order to invest in and empower women worldwide. It is our understanding that the church can give voice to those overlooked by policymakers. We participate enthusiastically in this work because we believe that the church is a powerful, transformative vehicle for the teaching, protection and enforcement of women's rights and gender equality when its constituents and leadership are informed and empowered.

The Commission on the Status of Women

The Commission on the Status of Women (CSW) is one of the original commissions from the founding of the United Nations (U.N.) in 1946. Each year meetings are organized around different themes. United Methodist Women partners with Ecumenical Women and NGO-CSW through worship, advocacy, and collaboration on important side events to inform the themes.

Each year, thousands of women from around the world gather at the U.N. in New York City during CSW. The event is an opportunity for women to influence the U.N.'s "concrete recommendations for governments, intergovernmental bodies, and civil society to implement at the international, national, regional, and local levels."

As one of the original U.N. commissions, CSW is to "evaluate progress on gender equality, identify challenges, set global standards and formulate concrete policies [recommendations] to promote gender equality and advancement of women worldwide." The primary outcome of the commission is a set of "agreed conclusions" that contain an analysis of the annual priority theme as well as concrete recommendations for governments, intergovernmental bodies, and civil society to implement at the international, national, regional, and local levels.

United Methodist Women also works with Church Women United, World Day of Prayer, the National Council of Churches, as well as the World Council of Churches and most of the general agencies of The United Methodist Church in one way or another.

Conclusion

Speaking of the role of United Methodist Women, Harriett Jane Olson summarized: "United Methodist Women has changed many times over our 140-plus years. We are an organization that has examined needs and found resources to meet them in many different ways. After all, it is the love of God that moves us. We know ourselves to be loved and we know that God's amazing love extends to the whole world. It is the hope that we have in God's good will for the world, and it is our faith in God through Jesus Christ that impels us into action, shaped and reshaped to respond to the needs of members and nonmembers around the world."

Information Guide

United Methodist Women's National Office
Membership and Leadership Development
475 Riverside Drive, Room 1501
New York, NY 10115
Tel. (212) 870-3725 (Membership) or 3629 (Leadership)

United Methodist Women Website
www.unitedmethodistwomen.org

United Methodist Women Online Community
www.umwonline.net

Twitter
www.twitter.com/UMWomen

Facebook
www.facebook.com/UMWomen

YouTube
www.youtube.com/UMWomen

Opportunities to Give
Online
www.unitedmethodistwomen.org/donate

Mission Giving Form
www.unitedmethodistwomen.org/give/forms

Resources

United Methodist Women offers many printed, audiovisual, and online resources. Go to www.unitedmethodistwomen.org to find current resources.

For Elected Leaders

- *The Book of Discipline of The United Methodist Church, 2012*
  The Book of Discipline includes the constitution of United Methodist Women. (Available from Cokesbury; call toll free 1-800-672-1789).
- *The Book of Resolutions of the United Methodist Church, 2012*
  The book lists official United Methodist Church position statements on a variety of social issues as approved by General Conference. (Available from Cokesbury; call toll free 1-800-672-1789).
- **United Methodist Women Handbook 2013–2016**
  The handbook provides information about organizing for mission at the local, district, conference, and jurisdiction levels. It includes guidelines about roles and responsibilities of leaders and relationships to other United Methodist organizations. The constitution and bylaws of United Methodist Women is included in this handbook.
- **New Unit Starter Kit**
  This kit will help you get started in organizing a local organization of United Methodist Women. You will also find in this kit resources to enrich your programs and information about online communities to stay connected with other sisters in mission.
- **New Member Packet**
  Get practical tips on how to become a member. The New Member Packet includes the following items: Sample **response** magazine, Charter for Racial Justice, Membership Joys brochures (in English, Spanish, and Korean), current resources catalog, and United Methodist Women in Mission booklet.
- **United Methodist Women PURPOSE Poster**
  (Available in English, Spanish, and Korean)
  Words of the PURPOSE of United Methodist Women are printed on a 24" X 36" full color, two-sided poster for display. One side is printed in one language, choose from English, Spanish, or Korean, and the other side is trilingual in English, Korean and Spanish.
- **Program Book for United Methodist Women** (published annually)
  A collection of monthly programs and special services for United Methodist Women members.
- **Resource Catalog**

For Members and Friends

- **Holy Bible: United Methodist Women (NRSV)**
  Featured are a presentation section for personalizing as a gift, a section with prayers and reflections on scripture passages through a mission lens, and journalizing suggestions and practical study ideas. Beautifully bound, including a satin ribbon marker.
- **Spiritual Growth Study** (published annually)
  (Available in English, Spanish, and Korean)
  This book is one of the three annual mission studies, written especially for United Methodist Women members. It includes a study guide for participants.
- **Mission Studies**
  United Methodist Women produces printed and audiovisual materials on a geographical mission theme and one a general mission theme. These are introduced in our denomination through Schools of Christian Mission, now called Mission u. Check United Methodist Women's website www.unitedmethodistwomen.org for current titles and descriptions.
- **Prayer Calendar** (published annually)
  A daily guide to prayer for mission workers and mission projects in the United States and around the world. Includes names, addresses, birthdays, special prayers, daily Scripture readings, testimonies and colorful pages showing mission projects around the world.
- **response magazine** (published 11 times a year)
  response is the voice of women in mission. Monthly Bible studies, stories of faith, and mission opportunities are just part of what you'll find. Call 877–881-2381 or visit www.unitedmethodistwomen.org/response to subscribe.
- **Charter for Racial Justice Policies**
  (Available in English, Spanish, and Korean)
  Contains the Charter for Racial Justice Policies for United Methodist Women, which also has been adopted as a resolution for The United Methodist Church.
- **Why Should I Get Involved in Social Issues?** (booklet)
  (Available in English, Spanish, and Korean)
  Learn how United Methodist Women in mission have been actively involved in social justice issues at the national and international level for more than 140 years and get involved.
- **Reading Program Catalog** (published annually)
  This free catalog describes Reading Program plans and books. Books are listed under each of the five mission emphases.
- **20 Questions About Women Organized for Mission**
  (Available in English, Spanish, and Korean)
  A brochure with answers to 20 frequently asked questions about United

Methodist Women, including its role in the church and in mission service, administration, organizational structure and more.

- **Join United Methodist Women**
  (Available in English, Spanish, and Korean)
  This brochure describes the process for becoming a member.
- **Membership Joys**
  (Available in English, Spanish, and Korean)
  This brochure highlights the benefits and commitments of membership, and provides a membership/pledge card with space to record pledged giving.
- **Mission Giving**
  (Available in English, Spanish, and Korean)
  Read in this brochure how you can be a part of the ever-growing mission of United Methodist Women locally, nationally, and internationally through the five channels of Mission Giving.
- **Major and Planned Giving**
  This brochure invites you to invest in the future of women, children, and youth through long-term giving.
- **Deaconess and Home Missioner**
  (Available in English, Spanish, and Korean)
  The brochure provides information for laity in The United Methodist Church who feel called by God to a full-time vocation in service with those who are marginalized and in need in the world today. There is an opportunity for them to be part of a supportive community in connection with The United Methodist Church.
- **United Methodist Seminars on National and International Affairs**
  (Available in English, Spanish, and Korean)
  United Methodist Seminars on National and International Affairs are committed to expanding concepts of mission through various educational sessions and hands-on experiences to provide deeper levels of understanding of important issues. The brochure provides information.
- *United Methodist Women News*
  Newsletter published quarterly for United Methodist Women.
- **United Methodist Women in Mission**
  (Available in English, Spanish, and Korean)
  This is a resource for new members, pastors, and all United Methodist Women and includes the biblical basis for our long heritage of mission, our purpose and ways of giving, equipping for leadership, and engagement in social issues.

AUDIOVISUALS
- **response** on CD: Highlighted articles from each issue available on a subscription basis. Call 877-881-2385 or visit www.unitedmethodist women.org/response to subscribe.

- *A Century+ In Mission* (CD)
  A Century+ in Mission is a multimedia presentation of the people, events, places, and actions of women organized for mission in the Methodist and Evangelical United Brethren traditions for 135 years.
- *10 Best Books of United Methodist Women History* (CD)
  This is a collection of 10 outstanding books on the history, programs, outreach, and personalities of millions of United Methodist Women involved in ministries with women, children, and youth for more than a century.
- *A Journey in Mission* (DVD)
  This DVD introduces United Methodist Women and the organization's mission work with women, children, and youth. Provides resources required to communicate mission stories.
- *United Methodist Women: Faith–Hope–Love in Action*
  Whether you are a new or longtime member, are considering joining, or know nothing about the organization, this membership video gives you a sense of the dynamics of United Methodist Women in mission.
  Also available: *The Assembly of United Methodist Women 2010, Live Joy and Mission Giving.*
- *Deaconess: Is This a Calling...*
  This 18-minute DVD illustrates the call, life, and varied ministries in both church-related and helping professions of the modern deaconess.
- *God's Transforming Mission*
  The 21st century presents major mission challenges Christians will confront in this century, including working with the world's poor, the impact of globalization, reconciliation among nations and peoples, and ongoing ministry to children and youth.
- *Resurrection Road* (with study guide)
  Resurrection Women are those who have chosen to follow the Risen Christ, in biblical times and today. This DVD offers individual and collective stories of Resurrection Women in the life of United Methodist Women in mission and includes a study guide.
- *Through the Corridors of Mission*
  This essential DVD tells the story of mission, with its triumphs and pitfalls, joys and missteps, urging the faithful to continue to be gospel-bearers, participating in God's passionate task of transforming the world.

NOTES

NOTES

NOTES

NOTES

NOTES

NOTES

Guidelines Resources

General Board of Church and Society, www.umc-gbcs.org, 202-488-5600; Service Center, 1-800-967-0880

General Board of Discipleship, www.gbod.org, 877-899-2780; Discipleship Resources, http://bookstore.upperroom.org, 1-800-972-0433; The Upper Room, www.upperroom.org, 1-800-972-0433

General Board of Global Ministries, umcmission.org, 1-800-862-4246 or 212-870-3600; E-mail: info@umcmission.org

General Board of Higher Education and Ministry, www.gbhem.org, 615-340-7400

General Board of Pension and Health Benefits, www.gbophb.org, 847-869-4550

General Commission on Archives and History, www.gcah.org, 973-408-3189

General Commission on Christian Unity and Interreligious Concerns, www.gccuic-umc.org, 212-749-3553

General Commission on Religion & Race, www.gcorr.org, 202-547-2271; E-mail: info@gcorr.org

General Commission on the Status & Role of Women, www.gcsrw.org, 1-800-523-8390

General Commission on United Methodist Men, www.gcumm.org, 615-340-7145

General Council on Finance and Administration, www.gcfa.org, 866-367-4232 or 615-329-3393

Office of Civic Youth-Serving Agencies/Scouting (General Commission on United Methodist Men), www.gcumm.org, 615-340-7145

The United Methodist Publishing House, www.umph.org, 615-749-6000; Curric-U-Phone, 1-800-251-8591; Cokesbury, www.cokesbury.com, 1-800-672-1789

United Methodist Communications, www.umcom.org, 615-742-5400; EcuFilm, 1-888-346-3862; InfoServ, 1-800-251-8140, E-mail: infoserv@umcom.org; *Interpreter Magazine*, www.interpretermagazine.org, 615-742-5441

United Methodist Women, www.unitedmethodistwomen.org; 212-870-3725 (membership)

Download the free training materials GUIDE TO THE GUIDELINES
and ORIENTATION WORKSHOP from www.cokesbury.com.

For additional resources, contact your Annual Conference office.

CPSIA information can be obtained at www.ICGtesting.com
Printed in the USA
LVOW12s1252270713

344876LV00003B/4/P